A Coal Miner's Son

A Coal Miner's Son
Life's journey to the edge and back

Garry Phillips

© Garry Phillips 2014 - All Rights Reserved.

Edited by: Robert Nahas
Written by: Writer Services, LLC
Book layout by: Chappell Graphix
Cover illustration by: Darius Molotokas

ISBN 10: 1942389000
ISBN 13: 978-1-942389-00-2

Printed and bound in the United States of America

Prominent Books and the sunburst compass logo are Trademarks of Prominent Books, LLC

Table of Contents

The Man On The Railing 1
Taken 5
Transition With My New Family 9
A Walk in My Shoes 13
Flood In The Valley 17
Fire In The Mountains 29
The Inbreeds 39
Trouble Strikes 53
Military Misadventure 65
Trouble Revisited 85
Getting Back On My Feet 99
Who Was The Man On The Railing? 101
Epilogue 105

Chapter One
The Man On The Railing

A man stood on top of the railing on a balcony some twenty-seven stories above the pavement. Just eighty pounds fully dressed, the wind caused him to sway in all directions. His arms hung sort of lifeless. It was remarkable that he was able to stay balanced at all, but there he stood, like a zombie.

Down below, the passers-by became curious over what others already there were looking up at. A crowd was beginning to accumulate.

He gazed down at them without any thoughts or considerations. Not even of the fact that he might land on some of them.

An unspoken anxiety began to build within the people watching as they began to realize what was actually happening beyond their earshot. The man on the balcony wasn't a worker cleaning something, or any other thing they could find logic with. He was a man about to end his life by plunging to his death.

Life had become too intolerable, unworthy of another day of pain and suffering, guilt and despair. There were eight people behind him who paid no attention to what was going on. They were too preoccupied as they waited for their next hit from the communal crack pipe. In aching numbness, they were all but dead, trying to maintain their own personal oblivion where nothing could be felt, nothing could be remembered.

Minutes before, the man on the railing had been huddled around his friends, smoking crack; as they did most every day in their pitiful existences. And without saying anything, he had gotten up and climbed onto the railing. And there he stood, without much thought.

He began to mumble as his lips, glued together with dried saliva, opened slightly on the right side of his mouth. Like a stroke victim, he said, "I'm gonna end my life right now." His heart started to beat fast, heavy and irregular.

Bobby, who was sitting on the balcony floor just below him, heard the words. Slow and distant, his incapacitated brain began to decipher the message. He was a crack friend of the man about to take his life. To him, Bobby was the coolest friend of them all. On the surface, the man's message informed of his next move. But it more importantly imparted an apology for cutting out and leaving his friend behind.

They often shared quarts of Knickerbocker beer and talked about better times that the future held. It was their only salvation from their ugly pasts, other than the drugs, of course. They confided in each other and sometimes even shared stories of their own tough experiences, their pain and fears they'd hoped would have been forgotten by then.

Bobby's brain finally figured out that his friend was about to jump to his death, "There'd be nothin' left of you if you jumped." But the man did not respond.

He tried to shake himself out of his stupor and talk his friend down. Mustering up some energy, he said, "They got a rehab!" Some of the others took their attention away from the pipe and looked, uncertain of what was happening but sensing the seriousness of the moment.

Bobby began to feel something he hadn't felt in many years. It was necessity. The fear of losing his friend caused his adrenaline to begin to pump through his veins, waking him up somewhat. He became afraid and wanted to stop what was about to happen. "Look at you, Man! You need rehab. You used to weigh 180 pounds, easy." Bobby got no response. Trying harder to reach him, he said, "I'm lookin' at you ... like you're close to death."

The man on the railing turned his head towards his friend with expressionless eyes as if to say "goodbye," and let himself tilt forward.

How anyone could bring their life to this extent is something we all might try to answer. But like a riddle that never allows for a clear answer, you can do nothing but guess.

It all seemed like chapters in a book, one leading to the next string in an unraveling rope of unjust occurrences and bad decisions and unfair outcomes....

Chapter Two
Taken

Things were good when I was very young. I had nice parents, and my brother Bruce and sister Andrea treated me fine. They were much older than I was—a good ten years or so.

The small space that dipped between the circle of mountains surrounding us was the entire world to me. Those hills were the Smoky Mountains, and we lived in the town of Coxton, Harlan County, Kentucky. Harlan was real small, smaller even than Mayberry on *The Andy Griffith Show*.

I was provided with food, shelter and a roof over my head. My mama even supplied me with extra amounts of love. She'd say you could never get completely filled up with it; there'd always be room for more, if only in my big toe. My papa, I could tell he loved me, though he never showed it as much, at least not in a conspicuous way. But there was no doubt he cared about me, very much.

One day, not long after my sixth birthday, a woman by

the name of Elizabeth came knocking at our door. She'd come visiting before, a few times. I knew her pretty well, myself, because she would always make a point to talk to me—a lot more than any other adult who wasn't family.

Most adults treated kids like they were stupid or unimportant, just by the way they ignored you or talked like you was a dog or something. But Elizabeth paid a lot of attention to me for some reason. I never minded much. She was okay. She even came to see me at school. Early schooling only went for half the day, and she picked me up and brought me home sometimes. I supposed friends of the family did those kinds of things.

Elizabeth said something and then things got quiet. My mama looked at me. She tried to hold her tears back, but anyone could see she was real upset. *Why's mama cryin'?* I wondered to myself. I continued playing with my dump truck, acting like I wasn't concerned, but I was.

A rumbling sound was running outside. I went to the window and saw an old, beaten pickup truck with a man in the driver's seat and what seemed like a truckload of kids. Every so often, it was about to stall, but the man in the driver's seat revved it back to life.

I noticed that my brother and sister had looks of concern on their faces. They wouldn't look right at me for more than a second or two before staring into space. There was a weird feeling that had built up in the room, and I started to feel it in the pit of my stomach. I was uncomfortable;

about what, I had no idea.

Elizabeth came over and knelt down right in front of me. "Boy, look at me."

I stopped pretending I was having fun with my truck and looked at her. She smiled nervously. I could tell because it wasn't her normal smile. I wasn't afraid, I just didn't know what was happening.

"I have something important to tell you, child." Her smile left her face. Then she brought it back again, this time more forced than before.

"I am your real mama."

"What?" My half-pint-sized heart began to beat hard.

"You're my child ... I'm your mother."

Saying nothing, I looked at the woman I had been raised by for ... since I could remember, and she strained her face in a lifeless smile as her welled-up eyes began to drain down her cheeks; her lips quivering.

"You're comin' home to your real family now," Elizabeth said. "Your real daddy got a job at the miners' camp and we can afford to bring you home now. He's out in the truck right now, waitin' to see you."

With no interest in seeing who was in the truck, I looked over to the man I had called Papa. He looked as stern as always, but a man can only do so much before his emotions show themselves in one way or another. His very tight lips walled a reservoir of sadness. He dared not try to speak and risk weakening the damn that held back the reservoir of tears.

I ran to him and hugged his legs. I wanted him to pick me up and protect me from what was happening, make it go away, stop what was happening. But he didn't move, nor did he put me in his arms.

He patted me on the back and said, "You need to be with your real family now. We love you, but we ain't your real family. A child needs to be with his real family."

He wasn't convincing, and it did not make things any better.

The lady, who was my biological mother, took my hands and peeled my arms from my papa and began to walk me towards the door. I started crying, and I could feel my immediate family all wanted to come to my rescue, but they knew it would only prolong what had to happen.

"No! No! No! No! Please! Don't take me away!... Mama!... Stop her!... Papa, help me!... Please! I don't want to go anywhere!" I grabbed the edge of the doorway with all my might, but Elizabeth pried my fingers on one hand and then the other; I couldn't hold on.

The screen door closed, the main door following after. I could hear my mama as she began to wail an agonizing sound. I looked back to see my papa holding her as I was carried towards the truck. My brother and sister ran off crying.

Chapter Three
Transition With My New Family

The transition to my real family didn't go very smoothly. I was homesick, and from sleeping without a pillow to all of the other abrupt changes in lifestyle, everything felt strange and unpredictable.

I was scared and felt out of place. Like a stray pup wolf wandering into a strange pack, my real blood brothers looked at me with sneers. They seemed very territorial. Maybe they thought I was an extra mouth to feed from a pot that held very little food to begin with.

Often, we were only allowed one spoonful of food for supper. My stomach used to ache and rumble in bed, which kept me awake for most nights.

I came to find out that my new (real) parents had a different way of bringing up children. My mother preferred a brown electrical cord for whipping and my father, a thick, wide miner's belt. They used to whip my brothers, but not me. Every time it happened, I'd hide under my bed and remain very quiet. With the sound of the screams and crying, I wanted no part of that. But once my little body came of age, per my parents' eyes, I became part of the lesson learning.

One day, I was outdoors, playing in our yard. The day had been nothing unusual; went to school, got pushed around some by my brothers, came home.... I was dribbling a basketball when I became a little bored. After all, having no hoop to try and shoot the ball through did not allow for hours of fun. I began bouncing the ball harder and harder, to see how high I could make it go. It was a lot of fun ... that is, until it hit a rock and ricocheted and went right through one of the windows in our house.

I stood there in horror, disbelieving what had just happened. My mother walked up and peered out through the frame of jagged glass. I stood frozen in fear.

"Get in here, boy!"

"I-I didn't mean it, ma'am."

"I told you to get yourself in this house, right now!"

I was nine years old when I got my first whipping. First from my mother and then later by my father.

I couldn't believe I was being beaten like that. It hurt so bad, I couldn't tell which was worse: a doubled-up electrical cord or the stiff minor's belt. My mother's cord gave two lashes for one thrashing, but the belt had weight to it and it covered a lot of area when it made contact with my skin. I was just skin and bones—not much meat to tenderize, and it hurt right down to the bone.

Transition With My New Family

I ran back to my original family and begged them to take me back, but they didn't.

My first whipping was a way of letting my brothers know that I was now fair game. They went from picking on me and shunning me, to beating me up. They started using me as their punching bag any time they felt like it. By now, things had gone from bad to worse.

The beatings from my real parents became fairly regular after the initial one, maybe about every couple of months. When my mother decided to give me a beating, I knew that when my father got home, tired and at wits' end with his patience, her complaints would cause him to pull his belt right from his pant loops, without hesitation. It was an automatic reaction, like touching a hot boiling pot and jerking your hand back from the heat, that belt came out just as quick.

Usually, if one of us were bad, we'd all get it just the same. The anticipation alone made up for having to go first. "Come here, boy!" was an address to oldest. He probably got it slightly worse because the belt would start out colder and a bit stiffer, stinging all the more. With each series of lashings, that belt, black from caked-in coal dust, got a little warmer and that much softer. Though that was splitting hairs, it was the only comfort I could think of to keep me from wetting my pants. But pain is pain, and as soon as it was my turn, my imaginary mind was immediately righted by reality.

I ran back to my original family's house many times. They'd let me stay there for a few hours, and though it pained my mama who raised me my first six years, every time I'd come there, she would have to send me back home because she couldn't keep me. The law always favors blood relatives. Things like love, caring and kindness had nothing to do with anything in a court of law.

I found ways to cope over time. If my mama wasn't home and I had nowhere else to go, as a survival mechanism, I would run away after my mother would whip me, so I wouldn't get it from my father too. I'm not saying I was an angel or didn't deserve some discipline now and then. I definitely had become a disagreeable child. But things got to the point where I'd run away to the woods or anywhere just to keep away and avoid another beating.

I'd run up into the mountains, deep into the woods.

Chapter Four
A Walk in My Shoes

Life in Harlan was as about as normal as it got in the South back then, with no real rift between blacks and whites.

Sure, people lived, literally, on "different sides of the tracks," but everyone got along. The miners, in particular, were completely integrated, with black men and white men working side by side. The same was true of school; there was no segregation of any kind, just one small schoolhouse all the kids attended.

The discipline at school wasn't all that dissimilar to home. No matter what color you were, the teacher would hit you if you were "dumb." I must have been the dumbest son of a gun in the county, because the teacher would hit me all the time. These were no love taps or fair warnings. She would hit us so hard we would see stars most of the time. No matter what it was, if it was wrong, you were dumb. If you were dumb, you were in for it.

If your face was dirty—bam! Stumble on the alphabet—

bam! Wrong answer to a math equation—bam!

One time we got back at her. Somebody put a banana peel on the floor for her to slip on. And it worked! Those funny comedy shows and cartoons had some truth to them, because those peels were definitely real slippery.

The one good thing about school was making friends. When you have to walk for some miles, as we did each day, it allowed for getting to know someone pretty well. And talking would make the long trek seem shorter. The roads were all made of dirt back then. We were so far from the mainstream of the world, it took three hours just to get to U.S. Highway 2. Sometimes we would take our shoes off and walk in our bare feet.

Later, as I looked back on those years, I'd remember those walks as the some of the best times of my childhood, and some of the best friends I ever made. Come to think of it, it was one of the few times in my life when I felt normal—just like everyone else.

Even when I wasn't in school, I used to walk for hours. Sometimes I'd find myself pretty high up in the mountains, where the dandelions grew all around. It was like looking at a bright yellow carpet stretching out for yards and yards ... maybe even a mile.

By far, they were one of my favorite flowers. I used to hold one in my hand and roll it between my fingers. It was like holding the sun or as if God was speaking. Not real words, but in a tongue translated by nature itself. More like a feeling than like anything specific. Like everything was going to be alright, or something like that. Sometimes, I'd run as fast as I could through a sea of them. It was like soaring over golden light so bright, you had to squint your eyes.

I was a real good climber, and I could work my way as high as I wanted. I might have been afraid of a lot of people and uncomfortable around them, but up there, I was just like an eagle or any other living thing, without conflict.

Little did I know at the time that I had become a pretty good botanist, learning how different plants looked and what they were for. I was able to spot lots of different kinds with my good eyesight. Sometimes I would search for wild greens, such as turnip greens, and pick them. Then I'd go door to door selling them. And I picked ginseng and sold them for folks who used it for medicinal purposes. It was a way of helping to put food on the table. To have some fresh cooked greens surely helped to fill my belly, especially during the scarcest times when the main course was just a spoonful.

A Coal Miner's Son

Chapter Five
Flood In The Valley

The fall rains had driven most of the colorful leaves to the ground. The few that remained hung dark and lifeless. The once plush and vibrant trees suddenly stood lanky and gaunt, posing a dreary atmosphere around the miners' camp. It had been an unusually rainy autumn, but we had no inkling of the catastrophe that was about to change all of our lives for years to come.

We were rejoicing in the garden produce we'd managed to grow after a long, hard summer, even though we would have to stretch it through the upcoming harsh winter we usually endured. My mother enjoyed her gardening very much, and I must admit, she was a pretty good cook when it came to soul food, and we had enough to go around.

Everybody was back in school, huddled around the old coal stove that heated the classroom, talking about all that happened over the past few months while we were on summer vacation, and of course joking and horsing around. The rain was still pounding down on the school's roof, and we had to raise our voices above the noise just to be heard. None of us even noticed the teacher when she came in, until she spoke.

"Listen up, kids. We are goin' to send you all home because the dam doesn't look too good and all of your families need to be packin' and movin' to higher ground. So when I let you go, you hurry on home and get to your parents. You all hear me now? Don't be wastin' time on getting right on home."

I had mixed feelings about the whole thing. For one, we weren't going to have school today, and that was exciting. Prolonged summer holidays would be a good thing. Another was that, at last, some real excitement and adventure would brighten our otherwise dull living. But underlying all of that was a feeling of dread that we might be in danger of losing everything we had called our own. My heart suddenly leapt to my throat. The look in the other kids' eyes seemed to solidify the fact that this wasn't just some fire drill.

I ran home to find my mother and father packing what little we had in bags that we could all carry. The whole town had been warned of the possibility of a flood, and all the miners had been sent home to prepare.

"Here, Garry. Take this," my father ordered, shoving a bag in my direction. "We gotta go up the mountain to that big old school up there, and we gotta go now. Fast." There was urgency in his voice that I had never heard before, and

Flood In The Valley

I knew we were all in trouble.

  I grabbed the bag and followed my family out the door into the chilly rain. There were a lot of families moving up the mountain to the school, and the small dirt road, now muddy, was packed with people, some in cars and some walking. I wondered why dad didn't take the old truck, and then I saw that traffic was backed up and it was most likely faster to walk. I turned around to take one last look towards my house. It wasn't much to look at, but it was my home, and I wondered if I would ever see it again. My father nudged me on.

  "Hurry up, son. We don't have much time."

  The bag I carried had mostly clothes and some stuff from the kitchen. It was heavy for a 13-year-old boy. Going up Coxton Mountain was steep, but we all had something to carry, so I couldn't ask for help with mine. I stumbled a few times and fell behind.

  "Wait," I yelled to the others.

  "Come on," my father replied. "The dam is about to break at any minute and we'll all be drowned."

  I gathered what was left of my strength and hoisted the bag to my shoulders. Fear of drowning alone must have injected new energy into my body as I struggled the rest of the way to the school.

  The whole town of over five hundred people seemed to be gathered there. I wondered how we would all fit in such a small school. One of the mining bosses met us and showed us to one of the schoolrooms where we were to stay for a while. I dropped my bag to the floor and collapsed on top of it, exhausted.

Then I heard a yell out in the schoolyard and dashed to my feet. Reaching outside, I stared down at the valley-town we had called home. A huge wall of water was coming down the river from the direction of the dam. We had gotten to higher ground just in time. I worried then that the water would also reach the school and looked over at my mother. She looked solemn and I could see that she had similar concerns. I could also see the sadness in her face as she watched the water devour her garden.

In fact, we all watched the town become a lake at the foot of the mountain, burying everything we had been familiar with for so many years. It then stopped rising, and I knew we were safe on the mountain.

I would have continued standing there, staring at the new lake and loss of homes, but the growling in my stomach reminded me that I hadn't eaten for hours, and I turned to go into the school. My mother, along with some other women, was already at a potbelly stove in one of the rooms putting something together for our family. It wasn't much, but it tasted good and dulled the ache in my stomach.

Living in the schoolhouse was exciting only for a few days before it became a struggle to exist. We didn't have school for a full year, and that seemed to make the time drag on for what seemed like an eternity. It was bitter cold inside the school building, and we huddled together to keep warm for the most part.

"When is someone coming to bring us food and water?" I asked my father.

"I don't know," he would say each time I asked.

"Maybe they don't know we are up here," I said. "Maybe we all gonna freeze to death or die starved."

The winter was settling in fast, and I didn't know if we would even have greens from the mountainside to add to the broth my mother gave us once a day. It was not too bad at first since many of the folks who came to stay had brought up canned food and packaged rice, beans and pasta with them. I went with a couple other boys to try to find wild greens to add to the meals, but the autumn freezes had killed most of them, and we often came back cold and empty handed. Finally, we gave up altogether.

There were five rooms in that schoolhouse and we crowded in as tight as we could. Sometimes I couldn't sleep at night and ended up sleeping during the day, crashing on our bags of belongings. But I felt luckier than the folks who stayed outside. Many of them just slept outside under the stars. Some had tents, but that didn't keep the cold out much. A few of the men brought empty barrels up to the school, and they lit fires in them using wood they found on the hillside. That helped to keep them warm some of the time and could be used to cook over too, I'd imagined.

I helped as much as I could, scouting for wood to burn in the potbelly stove and the barrels outside. Once, I found an English nut tree loaded with nuts and brought a bucketful down for all to eat. Made me a bit proud of myself to be contributing something.

We didn't have beds or mats to sleep on, so I curled up in one of the blankets brought from home and slept on the hard floor with the rest of them. It was cold, and I woke up in the morning stiff and sore. I didn't dare complain to my mother. I could see she was just as sore as I was and maybe even worse. I wondered if it would ever end.

Sometimes I would go to the ridge and look down at the valley lake hoping it was gone and we could find our house still standing there. But no such luck. The lake showed no signs of getting smaller, and I would find tears welling up in my eyes and wishing I could just wake up from this terrible nightmare. Seemed that we were forgotten by the rest of the world and would all finally die of starvation.

One day, as I looked out at the lake, I saw several boats coming across the river. I ran to the school house shouting at the top of my lungs, "Someone's coming. Someone's coming!"

Most of the men hadn't gone back to working in the mines, which, for the most part, had been flooded out, and they were all there to run down to greet the newcomers. We had been up in the school building for three weeks now without word from anyone, and we were all very excited to see someone new, hoping that it was good news and not just some more people to feed. Lord knows we had little to eat as it was.

Then we saw that it was the Red Cross and were we ever glad to see them! It seemed that they had brought colder weather with them, and our first gentle snow started to fall as we helped them from the boats. It felt like Christmas as we unloaded boxes and bags. It was amazing how such simple things could get one excited! Especially when you have done without. Some of us got mats to sleep on and blankets to keep us warm at night. And of course, they brought large cans of food, which we all pitched in to stack on shelves at one side of the classroom that we called the "kitchen". They brought us rice, pasta, beans and a few large pots to cook in.

Some of the women went straight to cleaning up the place. It was filthy with so many of us living there, seemingly on top of each other. Somehow the renewed hope got us all to thinking that we could do something to make living a bit more comfortable. We were all laughing and joking around with more energy than we had had in weeks.

My father came and got me after us boys had finished stacking the food on the shelves. "Come outside to help the guys, son."

I followed him outside to where the outhouses were. The men had dug some rather deep holes in the ground, and someone had found some boards stacked out back and had built some makeshift latrines. We helped to move them over the holes in the ground. This would be better, I thought. It was tough waiting in line when the need arose; especially for us kids. Most of the time, we boys would just hike up into the mountain for a bit to relieve ourselves, but I guess it was harder for the girls. And with winter nearly on top of us, that was going to be more difficult for everyone.

The Red Cross folks only stayed for the afternoon and had to leave, promising us they would be back with more stuff. I was hoping that I could go with them, but I knew I couldn't really leave the rest of the family behind, so I stood there with everyone else, waving goodbye as the last boat left the shore to go back up the river.

"Do you think they will come back?" I asked my father. He shrugged and frowned, but said nothing. I had the courtesy to say nothing more and just crossed my fingers behind my back. I was thinking we would never see them again.

The next few days were busy with everyone putting order into the schoolhouse and the area around. New wood was chopped and stacked against the outer wall, and the barrels used for heating outside were dumped of their ashes and prepared for the upcoming colder days. We kids were put to work and had no real time for play. At night, I was so tired that I collapsed on the mat I shared with one of my brothers and didn't move an inch until daybreak.

It was a few more weeks before the Red Cross came again, and by that time, we had started giving up hope once more. The food had been devoured a bit too fast with everyone there, and the mice and rats in the building had gotten into the rice and pasta. Again, the house started to look filthy with rodents running here and there between the classrooms. The lake stayed where it was, and the rains still came until it got too cold some days and it turned into snow. The only good thing about the rain was that it was collected in pots set outside, which gave us some drinking water and water for cooking. Once it snowed, we had to wait until there was enough to melt on the stove inside. If I ever thought I had had it rough in the miners' camp, I knew it was not nearly as tough as I was having it now.

Once the snows came, we were stuck inside. That year, there was a lot of snow, and we spent all of winter held up in that schoolhouse. The days dragged on endlessly, and the only way to make them tolerable was to crawl under a blanket and sleep as much as I could. Finally, I was slept out and joined some of the other kids in games of checkers with crayoned cardboard circles on a makeshift checkerboard. One of the men started whittling chess pieces out of wood, and we sometimes watched him carving the hours away.

By spring, I was sick and tired of being inside and ventured up the mountain a ways. It felt good to get away from all those people.

From the top of the mountain, I could see the lake still sitting down in the hollow. But it looked smaller by quite a bit. I wondered if I could see my house and looked long and hard. At first, I thought I saw the roof and then realized it was only a branch in the water. There was nothing there yet.

Later, I asked my mother if she thought we would move back into our house when the lake was gone. "No," she said. "I reckon our house has gone down the river and piled up somewhere on some bank."

Although I thought so as well, I still hoped there would be something left that I would recognize as my old home. Even if the house were gone, would I see the big tree I used to climb or the garden mom planted? Maybe not. But in any case, anywhere might be better than where we were at that point in time.

I hiked over to a waterfall that we boys had stumbled across earlier that month. I had been told by my father that a couple boys had drowned there a few years earlier when the current had caught them and pulled them under. He didn't want me to go there after I had told him that we had found the falls, but I did anyway. I was a good swimmer and so were the other boys, and we knew all about the current.

When I got there, some of my friends were lying on a flat stone at the side of the waterfall, their black and white bodies shimmering side by side, stark naked, warming in the sun. They saw me coming and called to me. Once I got to them, I stripped off my clothes and dove into the basin at the foot of the falls, watching out for the current created by the falls. The water was still chilly and I came up gasping for air. The other boys jumped in, and together we swam under the falls where we could perch on a large rock and enjoy the falling water on our bodies. For once in a long time, I felt clean again, even though I shivered from the cold. Later, we stayed on the rock outside of the waterfall, sunning ourselves until the sun heated up our bodies and the chill was gone. Then we threw on our clothes and hiked back to the school.

The summer came with its flies and heat, and some of the men had gone out hunting to see if they could kill some game for the meager meals we were eating. For once, we boys were out playing catch with some baseball that we had found in the school earlier that winter, when it was too cold to go outside with it. I had noticed that the lake had gone down quite a bit and heard that the dam had been fixed. My father was talking to other men and I overheard them.

"The lake has just about gone," my dad said. "But there isn't anything left of the town. They'll have to rebuild from start."

"What are they gonna use?" one of the men asked. "There ain't any lumber down there or anywhere else."

"I think the mining company is planning to build us some decent houses," another of the men said.

"Not much of a road left," my father said. "They might have to build some road first. That might take another year."

My heart sank as I thought about it. Another year in this god-forsaken schoolhouse was just too much to consider. Could we survive another year? I just knew that I couldn't, and yet, where could I go? I resigned myself to another year of misery.

Then one day, I woke up to hear a large rumble echoing in the valley. I dashed outside and joined the other boys staring down at a large bulldozer in the valley. The mining company had put together a makeshift road, good enough for some heavy trucks to bring in some lumber and building supplies. Soon they would be building homes for us again.

Then the mine bosses came to grab some of the men to work, building houses, while others went back to work the mines once they reopened. I wondered if the kids would start school in the fall. By this time, I was only too eager to get back to studying, and eager to move out of the crowded schoolhouse.

Chapter Six
Fire In The Mountains

The summer came hot and dry that year. With no plumbing and no clean water, the whole place stunk, and the flies buzzed around endlessly, getting into our food and even bothering our faces. We drank rainwater when it rained, but that was seldom. Some people drank the creek water, but after some folks got sick and died, my mother insisted we get water from the waterfalls. So we ended up bringing water down from the falls, which was three or four miles away up in the hills. That was a lot of hard work; us all carrying pails up the mountain and coming back, sweating like pigs on a hot summer day with no shower or bathtub filled with water to wash off with. Sure, there was a basin of water that we could use to take a sponge bath, but it wasn't as cool.

That was also the summer my family moved to the pig farm. It wasn't fancy, but it seemed like a palace after the crowded schoolhouse. My mother tried to get her garden going again, but it didn't go too well. There just wasn't enough rain. No matter what my mother did to try to get the plants to grow, most of them just wilted in the heat and died. A lot of the families' pets in the area died of starvation and our pigs didn't do much better. Although we could eat the female pigs when they died, we couldn't eat the dead boars because they tasted bad. It was a hard summer.

Once more, we had little food in the house, and we felt neglected by the state. Even when we tried to get food stamps, we were turned down. I wondered if it would always be like this—going to bed hungry most nights.

"You gotta have faith in the Lord," my father would say. "He is watching and will take care of us all, somehow." My parents' faith kept us all going strong at times like these. Sometimes it seemed that was all we had.

My father wrote letters to the government, and he got us kids to write some, too. We never heard back at first. It was like we were a forgotten people in that mining camp back there in the hills.

One of our neighbors suggested that we do a protest march into Harlan and let someone know what was happening in our valley. They all got together and took a vote. Only the older folks and sick ones voted yes. So, hoping to get help with getting drinking water, we protested in Harlan with picket signs that I helped draw up with a marker pen on cardboard brought back from the grocery store. We would walk the four miles into Harlan and up to the courthouse. Three times a week we would go, all three hundred of us.

One time, as we approached the courthouse, a riot started. I had no idea who started it—whether it was one from our group or an outsider living in Harlan. Someone started throwing rocks at the courthouse. My father gathered our family up and pulled us over to the side.

"What's happening?" I asked.

"Just a bit of bad feelings," my father said. "We are going to stay out of it. Can't afford to be in trouble."

I watched as police came to settle the riot down, and then we were told that if we didn't go back home and stop this marching, the judge would put us all in jail. My father laughed.

"Listen to this," he said. "The jail only holds twenty people and there are three hundred of us."

We did go back home, but that didn't slow us down any. Not paying any attention to the threat, we just kept on marching, week after week. The men even refused to work at the mine, and it finally paid off.

The city of Harlan eventually sent a fire truck with a big tank out to bring us water. It did its rounds from house to house delivering water to any who were home at the time. If you were gone for any reason, you would be out of luck that week and without water, so we always made sure someone was at the house that day.

The first time it came around to all the houses, we were

excited, but when we saw the brownish water, we were disappointed.

I looked at my mother. "I'm not drinking that," I said.

However, my mother boiled the water and we drank it anyway. Tasted terrible. We filled the bathtub so we could have water for washing and flushing the indoor toilet. A lot of the older folks got sick and died from drinking the water, and we just buried them in holes in the ground.

The government finally sent some people out to check on the place and see how they could put in a sewer system. But it would take a total of thirteen years before the first tap could be turned on to give us fresh water.

To get away from all the troubles at home, my brothers and I used to fish down at the Cumberland River whenever we could. We'd use sticks for poles and crawfish that we'd catch with our bare hands. Or we'd dig up worms or find grubs under rocks. By this time, I'd started to get a little more meat to my bones, so fighting with my brothers had become a little more fair. Now, when I fought back, they felt it, and there's nothing like a good right hook to the jaw to earn some respect. Whether it was actually respect or just good sense to avoid getting more bruised up, they stopped picking on me as much as they used to. They even got to the point of treating me like a brother.

I also used to do a lot of hiking in the mountains with my cousin, Jeremy. Not only did we revisit the waterfall to do our usual dip in the basin and settle under the refreshing falls itself to feel the splash of water on our heads, but we also hiked deeper into the hills. Sometimes we visited the old schoolhouse where we had stayed during the flood. A lot of the folks had moved into homes of some sort and some moved away, and the place was empty and neglected. We didn't stay there long, as the place itself held nothing but bad memories. Later on, the building would be torn down. It had definitely seen better days.

One time on a hot fall day, we decided to take a different route through the mountains and followed a path deeper than we had ever gone. We had seen some buck tracks and followed them back in the hills hoping to see a beautiful deer. It surprised us to find some chicken coops and goat farms up there that we had never known about. We watched them from a distance and were hesitant to get closer. I had heard some wild stories about the hillbillies who lived up in the mountains and wasn't sure if these were them or not. At any rate, I didn't want to bump into any of their kind. I was sure I wouldn't come back alive.

There were areas on the mountainside that must have been used for grazing the goats. Mostly grass grew there, and this summer, because it was pretty dry, the grass had turned into hay. It rustled under our feet as we walked across.

"What's that guy doing over there?" My cousin pointed to a guy at the far end of the meadow. We were in plain view, but the man had his back turned to us. Looked like he was trying to light a fire, and we could see flashes of flame. He must have heard us because he turned and raised his gun.

"Run!" I yelled. "He's got a gun."

I heard the bullet whiz by us as we ran.

"Oh, no," Jeremy shouted at me. "He's shooting at us!"

We took cover behind some trees, and it was then that we saw the fire had gotten out of control. Whatever that guy was doing would be forever a mystery; we just knew we had to get out of there, and quick. It was amazing how fast the fire spread across the grassy hill!

Instead of running toward home, we were forced to take off in a different direction, away from the crackling of the fire, and away from the guy shooting at us. It was a mistake, we soon found out. The fire was coming at us and we had come to a sixty-foot cliff with nowhere to go but over it.

I stared down at the jagged rocks that sat at the base of the cliff. No way was I going to jump over and trust that I would come out alive. No chance of that. But I heard the fire coming closer and knew I had to do something quick.

"Come over here," I yelled. "We can crawl down part of the cliff here and cling to the side while the fire goes over us." It was a daring chance and no promise of survival, but there was no other way.

We carefully slipped over the edge and got a toehold on some rocks. Slowly, we made our way down the cliff with

Fire In The Mountains

the fire crackling louder and louder overhead as it raced towards us.

"We gotta go lower," I said. "It's getting too hot. We'll roast alive. There is a ledge down about twenty feet to the left. Let's see if we can reach it. Jus' take it easy going across and down."

I could hear the flames exploding the evergreens at the top of the cliff, and a flaming branch came shooting over the cliff towards us. Hugging the wall of the cliff, I closed my eyes and whispered a prayer. The tip of a falling branch caught my shirt as it went by, and I nearly lost my balance. I felt the heat but nothing caught on fire, and I was fine for the moment.

"That was close," Jeremy said. "I'm almost at the ledge. Keep coming, Garry."

More flaming branches came flying down, and a small bush that grew on the side of the cliff between me and the ledge where Jeremy stood waiting burst into flames. I could barely see him through the smoke pouring out of the bush.

"Stay there," shouted Jeremy. "There's another smaller ledge about five feet down from where you are, but it will be tricky getting there, and it's skinny. You gotta go slow and keep tight to the cliff."

I could feel the heat waves from the fire rush by me pushed by gusts of wind, and I started coughing on the smoke. The force of the cough loosened the rock my foot was on and I felt myself slipping. Three feet down, I slid, face scraping against the rocky cliff-side. Then my foot hit something solid.

"Your foot is on a small tree branch," Jeremy said. "Only two more feet and you will be on the ledge."

I was afraid to move, and my cheeks felt they had been sanded raw. Finally, I let myself slide another two feet and felt the security of a ledge. It sure was narrow, and I had to cling to the rock to maintain my balance. At least I was away from the heat of the fire and the branch missiles that showered down like fiery rain.

Looking over toward Jeremy, I saw a way I could get across by stepping on small bushes that grew out from the cliff-side. I would be fine as long as the plants were well rooted. Slowly, I stepped across to the first plant. It held and I was fine, and that encouraged me to take another step to the next one. Bit by bit, I inched my way to the wider ledge that my cousin was on. He reached over and grabbed my arm to steady me when I got close enough. I smiled back at him. Now what? I wondered.

We clung to the cliff-side until the firestorm passed by, then half-slid and half-climbed down to the bottom of the cliff itself. The valley there had escaped the forest fire so far, and we took off running down a path toward our own valley. We hoped that the wind wouldn't change its course and come back at us again.

As we entered our valley, we saw the fire trucks coming.

Fire In The Mountains

They stopped at the foot of the mountain, but it was plain they couldn't do anything else. There was no access to the fire. We slowed down until we passed them and then took off running again.

I was never so glad to see the pig farm in my entire life, and we ran into the farmhouse out of breath.

"You smell like smoke, son." My mother stared at me.

"Some guy was shootin' at us," I explained. "He was doin' somethin' up there but I don't know what. His fire went out of control and nearly caught us."

"There's folks up there with goats and chickens," my mother said. "The firemen can't get to them in the mountains. I think they're goners. Sure glad you got out."

Me too, I thought.

The fire burned itself out after destroying hundreds of acres. With that went the goats, chickens and farmers. I felt sorry for those people up there. They didn't have a chance. Neither did the goats and chickens.

Black Mountain sat untouched by the fire, and I still went hiking there. But I stayed closer to home, going only part way up the mountain to see Amanda, a friend who I liked to visit. We would watch movies late into the night on the weekends. This one weekend I went up there would be the most frightening experience I had ever had since the day I was born.

A Coal Miner's Son

Chapter Seven
The Inbreeds

It was real late. We had watched quite a few movies back-to-back and eaten a few bowls of buttered popcorn. Amanda yawned and I knew it was way past time to go. The clock showed one a.m. when I passed it in the kitchen on my way to the front door. I looked out the doorway and stared into the thick blackness that made you wonder whether anything was even there or not.

I felt a nervous quiver in my stomach. "Awful dark out there ... I'm gonna be in so much trouble ... not even a moon tonight. Man!" I dreaded coming home late. I knew my father would be mad, fueled extra by my mom's worrying, which she would make well-known by the way she'd look at him. Even though I was fifteen, they still treated me like a child, and although I hated it, I knew better than to cross them up. All the whippings I got as a child taught me not to. Running out of things to say, my stalling tactics quickly grew old.

"You can't stay," was all that Amanda said.

I let the door close behind me as she turned the light out. The night seemed to swallow me up in its darkness. I stayed there for a moment, waiting for my eyes to get used to the darkness, but it was pitch black out and it didn't get much better. *I gotta get goin*, I thought. *Already in enough trouble being so late.* The autumn nights were starting to get cooler and I began to shiver, wishing I had thought to bring a jacket earlier.

It was four miles to home. I groped and stepped carefully for about a mile without mishap before I saw the bridge up ahead. It had the only streetlight for miles so I quickened my pace and felt a little more at ease. By the time I got to the bridge, I could hear an old rumbling car coming my way. I stood under the light so they could see me.

The car stopped right in front of me. "Wanna ride?" The voice had an odd twang to it and I wondered what part of the country he was from.

I thought I was lucky to be getting a ride until I saw that the car had no doors and the four big men inside didn't look too friendly. Then I got real scared when one of the guys jumped out of the car, waved a gun at me and said, "Git in d' car, boy."

They squeezed me into the middle, then the driver floored it and the car took off, loud as could be. An overwhelming stink of exhaust fumes, burning oil and BO filled my nostrils.

I began to panic as we skidded around the next corner,

me leaning on the man to my left as he laughed out loud and hung halfway out of the car. The driver never took his foot off the gas pedal. The man to my right was pushing on the both of us. The car straightened out again and I felt like I was going to vomit. I figured that would get me into more trouble, so I did all I could to hold down all that popcorn I'd had at Amanda's house. Though I was breathing heavy, I didn't say a word.

It wasn't long before the paved road turned into dirt, and I still had no idea where we were going. All I knew was that I had to get out of there before these inbreeds killed me. I had heard horror stories of how crazy these guys were and how they had no respect for anyone or anything, including the law.

The guy on my left was rubbing my arm, trying to rub off the black of my skin. He kept cursing when nothing rubbed off. The guy on my right had the gun but must have figured I was trapped and he wouldn't need to use it, so he tucked it away. I was so scared I was shaking and the sweat was pouring off me. From what I'd heard about the mountain inbreeds, taking the life of another human being meant nothing to them. Even the cops left them to themselves.

I grew more unstable as we went further up into the mountains, knowing that even if I were to escape somehow, I wouldn't know my way out of this terrain. Finding my way back home, especially in this darkness, seemed impossible. I didn't know if I should take the chance of running or hold out for some kind of miracle. Either way, things didn't look good for me. I knew no one would even find my body if they killed me.

The stench from these people was overwhelming. It wasn't just body odor from unwashed bodies; their breath stunk from mouths that had been grossly neglected for years—with the few teeth they had left rotting away. Between the smell and the bumpy car ride, the nausea grew more difficult to control.

We had gone quite a ways into the Black Mountains, by my guess, at least twenty miles up into the mountain range. But when my chance came, I took it. There were some ruts in the road, and as the car slowed to avoid them, the guy rubbing my arm let go of me to hold on. I scrambled over him and threw myself out the open door. One of the guys grabbed my shirt and I heard it rip as I toppled onto the ground.

Then I got up ran as fast as I could. I didn't want to lose a second's lead, so didn't even look behind. I just kept running with all of my might.

At first I tried to stay on the dirt road so as to be able to keep my directions straight, but then the guy with the gun started shooting at me. Bullets zipped by me, and I veered into the woods, terrified. I heard more bullets whiz by my head like some angry bumblebees.

I couldn't see a thing in the darkness, and as I ran

through the woods I kept running into trees and tripping over rotting logs, roots and stones. I was getting scraped and cut from tree branches, and I knew if I didn't slow down some I'd wind up twisting my ankle in a hole in the ground; I might even step off a cliff and get myself killed. I tried to keep parallel to the road so I wouldn't get my directions too confused. Worse case scenario, I would be able to follow the long, winding road out of these back mountains. At first, it was easy to stay clear of my pursuers; they had turned the car around and I could hear it rumbling down the road. But then I heard some sounds crashing through the trees and I knew that least two of them had left the car to come after me on foot. They had some kind of light and I could see it flashing here and there through the trees. My heart was beating so loud and hard, I thought they would be able to hear it, and the adrenaline was pumping through my body. I knew just what it was like to be a hunted animal.

While working to create distance between them and me, I thought about how I was in more trouble now because I still wasn't home yet and my parents wouldn't stand for that. But that was the least of my worries, and a good beating right now would be much more desirable than the fate I was facing at the moment.

I could hear them quietly talking back and forth. Sometimes they made animal or bird sounds, like they were stalking prey. I snuck through the woods more slowly now, trying not to make any noise. I didn't even see the stream until I walked right into it. I managed not to call out as my feet hit the cold water, but there was no mistaking the loud splash.

"Git 'im!" came a voice to my right. I could hear the men running right towards me. Still too dark to see, I could only suppose they were all together and not surrounding me. That's when I realized their light was no longer flashing. Maybe it had gone out! I didn't have time to think about it, though. I had to lose them and try to figure out where I was. Otherwise I was gonna die there.

I still had no idea where I was. But there was one thing I did know, and that was I would rather die lost in the woods than by the hands of an inbreed.

I forced my wet, exhausted legs to keep going, running out of the stream and away from the direction of the voices. A few minutes later, I heard water. I had come across a creek. I quickly waded into the cold water, which came up to my waist, and fought my way to the other side. Then I took off running again until I slammed into a tree that had fallen over. My foot slid into a crevice between the branches and got caught. I could hear them coming and panicked, trying to pry my foot loose. It was completely stuck!

They were close now, so I got down closer to the tree, trying to hide in the maze of branches. Just then, I heard footsteps coming toward me, then whispered voices. All four men were walking right for me! I struggled to quiet my breathing though my winded body was gasping for more air. I could now hear the leaves crunching just a foot or so away from me, could even smell their putrid body odors again. I closed my eyes tight and held my breath. Holding perfectly still, I prayed they wouldn't see me. I was thankful that on that day I had not put on any cologne, which would have been my certain death. They stood there a few minutes, then grew frustrated and staked walk off, crashing through the brush further up the creek. I stayed where I was for another fifteen minutes to be sure they were gone and then tried to free my foot. It wouldn't come loose and I was afraid to work it too hard in case I'd sprain it, or even worse, break my ankle.

Ready to give up, I shifted my cramped body into a better position and, as luck would have it, my foot slipped out of my shoe and I was free. I reached down to get the shoe, but it had disappeared into the tangle of branches and underbrush beneath the fallen tree. It was gone!

There was no time to worry about it, though; I had to get moving and get out of that place in case the inbreeds came back.

I moved away from the creek and climbed over a small hill, hoping to lose them for good. Several times, I stepped on something sharp and knew I'd cut my foot, but I couldn't stop. I kept on moving through the forest, hoping that I was going the right way home.

A Coal Miner's Son

The eastern sky was beginning to show some light and I realized that morning was on its way. That would make it easier for me to see, but also make me more visible to the inbreeds. Not good! I would have to find some place to hold up in until nighttime came again.

I decided to climb up the mountain a ways to see if there were any caves or hiding places. I could still hear them crashing around through the trees below and so I climbed treacherously higher, feeling my way through the semi-darkness up a small cliff. Then I found it—a cave that was very shallow with some bushes in front. I carefully slid into the cavity, hoping there would be no snakes or other dangerous creatures. Pulling my legs in closer to my body and behind the thick bush, I realized how sore my muscles were. I could also feel how tired I was.

I could no longer hear the others and hoped they had given up and gone home to sleep. But my wish wasn't fulfilled. I heard a noise at the foot of the cliff, then their heavy raspy breathing. My own breathing was coming hard and fast, and I had to slow it down so they wouldn't hear me. By taking deep, slow breaths and holding them for a count of five, I was able to stop my panting. They were coming closer. As I curled myself into a tight ball, I remembered being told how the inbreeds were excellent hunters and knew the mountains like the back of their hands. All I could do was pray they didn't know where this shallow cave was.

A couple times they came very close to where I was. I swear I could have reached out in the dark and touched their legs. All they had to do was squat down and they could have grabbed me. But, thank the Lord, they didn't have the common sense to do that.

Finally, I heard them moving away from me. I waited a few more minutes then stretched out my legs. That's when I realized I had ripped my pants in places and the cuts on my skin were beginning to sting. Some were still oozing sticky blood that tickled my leg as it dripped down to my feet and into my remaining shoe. There was nothing I could do about that, I figured. I just wanted to live to see another day. The thought of what those inbreeds would do if they caught me was too much to even think about. I just had to focus on getting out of those back mountains.

There was no use in leaving my hiding place and being seen in the coming daylight, so I decided to stay until nightfall. Perhaps they would give up by then so I could find the road and head off for home.

I don't know when I fell asleep, but sleep I did. I guess the running tired me out so much that I didn't even hear the rain that fell during the day.

It was afternoon when I woke up. The only sounds came from the birds in the trees, and I figured that was a good sign that the inbreeds had gone home. Still, taking no chances, I stood slowly from my hiding place and looked around. I could see a silver ribbon of a river in the far distance and hoped it was the Cumberland River. That would give me some idea of where home might be. I couldn't see the dirt road, so that wasn't going to be any help. I didn't see any houses nearby where I could go for help either. But then, any houses in these parts might just belong to the inbreeds, and that would be like walking right into the lion's den.

I stretched my legs. They were so stiff that I thought it might take a while before I could get them moving. But my stomach growled, and I knew I had to find something to eat soon. So off I went, at first sliding a bit down the wet rock to the base of the cliff, then walking a bit more quickly down through the forest towards the next hill.

The fear that the crazy inbreeds might decide to hunt for me some more kept me going. As I walked, I was also on the lookout for something edible since I was getting weak with hunger. But I didn't come across anything before night fell, and it was dark once again.

Fortunately, the sky had a billion stars and a sliver of a moon, so it wasn't as dark as the night before. I could at least see what was in front of me, but I still had no idea where I was or if I was even heading in the right direction. I hadn't seen or heard the others for the rest of the day, so I might have let my guard down some.

It was a mistake that almost cost me my life. I was coming over the top of a hill when they nearly spotted me. They were searching for me down in the valley and once again had a flashlight with them. I was glad they didn't have dogs, 'cause then I would have been a goner! Quickly backtracking my steps around the hilltop, I headed back the other way. By now, I had no idea where the Cumberland River ran. I was so turned around and confused, but I thought if I could just keep going, I'd sooner or later come to some place that was familiar to me. I also knew that I could be going further into the mountains, and that would take me closer to the inbreeds' home or just be lost forever.

My feet hurt, especially the one without a shoe, and the mosquitoes were eating me up alive. I was so hungry, I could have eaten just about anything. In fact, I tried some leaves, but they were so bitter. I choked on them and couldn't get them down. I heard the sound of a waterfall, but I couldn't get close enough to get a drink.

The inbreeds would not give up. I spent the night dodging them and trying not to walk in circles. By morning, I was thirsty, tired and starving. I think I was dying a little. I had very little energy in me ... very little life. I almost cried out with joy when I found an English nut tree and pulled some of the nuts from the branches. Using a stone, I cracked them open and devoured the tasty nut meat inside. It was only a little and such a teaser to my appetite, but it did take an edge off the hunger pangs.

By mid-morning, I had lost the inbreeds, or they had given up, but I still had no idea where I was. I saw some shacks on the side of a mountain, but was too scared to go there without knowing who they belonged to. The closest house had a bit of a garden out back. Didn't look like anyone was home, so I took a sharp rock I had collected from the creek and used it to cut some rhubarb. Only had a few stalks that tasted horribly bitter. I ate them anyway.

I was getting weaker and knew I had to find someone to help me get home. One house I came across had an old man sitting out on the front porch smoking a pipe. He could be anyone as far as I knew and could kill me just like any other mountain man. I took a chance. I saw a dog at his side and hoped it was friendly.

I walked up to his porch and said, "Please, sir. Don't kill me."

He looked at me and asked, "Where you comin' from, boy? I ain't gonna kill ya."

I told him the predicament I was in and where I lived, and he shook his head in disbelief.

"You know, you could have gotten yo'self killed? You are one lucky boy. Nothin' but crazy peoples up in them hills. And they would have killed you fo' sure if they'd caught ya."

He took me into his house and got me something to eat. Then he started his old car and we got in.

"It's at least twenty miles to the highway from here," he said, "and another ten miles to your house."

I wasn't sure if I trusted the old man, but I had to take a chance.

Within the hour, I was home. My parents took one look at me, and any anger about me being gone drained from their faces. After thanking the old man, they rushed me to the hospital where I was treated for dehydration, lacerations and insect bites. I thought I was done with the ordeal… until the nightmares began. For weeks afterward, I woke up every night, screaming in terror, thinking I was still being chased by those crazy, evil men in the woods.

A Coal Miner's Son

Chapter Eight
Trouble Strikes

After the frightening adventure with the inbreeds, I'd thought I was done with danger. But, sure enough, it found me again three years later when I turned nineteen. In fact, from that point on, it seemed like there was trouble everywhere I turned.

We still lived in a small mining town where whites and blacks got along. Many of my friends were white, but that year was a bad one for the blacks in Kentucky. It had been at least ten years since Martin Luther King, Jr. was assassinated, but there was still racial unrest with segregated schools, buses and public places. We'd always felt sort of immune to these events, but then we heard that the KKK had formed a group somewhere in our neighborhood. We were on the watch for these guys and my mother told me not to wander too far. But boys will be boys, as she put it later, and I hiked around a lot with my two brothers and our cousin Jeremy. At that time, I felt indestructible, like most young men of that age. I was also taking acid and smoking weed at that time, and the drugs gave me a false sense of security.

It was during our wanderings that we found an old sawmill that had been abandoned some years earlier. The sweet scent of sawdust and the feeling of it under my feet drew me back to it day after day, just for the sheer pleasure of it. Sometimes we would wander around the place looking for something new. But mostly we just sat around and smoked weed, talking about the earlier adventures we had had, or about girls at school. It was a carefree summer and none of us had a job or anything better to do. Like my mom always said, we were just sitting there idle, inviting trouble to find us.

One day, we went to the sawmill after dinner, instead of the afternoon like we usually did. As we approached, we saw other people were there, so we hid out in the woods to see who they might be. They were dressed funny, with white robes and pointed hoods that covered their faces. We'd never seen anything like it.

"Who's that?" my brother asked, and I told him I figured they were the KKK and we had better not mess with them.

We watched, mystified, as they performed some sort of ceremony involving the burning of a cross. I had heard enough about the KKK to be scared of them, but I had to admit I found them interesting too. After a bit, we left without them noticing us. It wasn't long before we realized that they had weekly meetings at the old sawmill, and we

Trouble Strikes

would creep up to the place and watch them from a safe distance.

And it didn't take much longer to get bored with the whole thing and wish for some action. I guess that's what made us think of taking our BB guns with us. We felt mischievous in those days, especially after doing drugs and spying on them for some time. They seemed harmless in their funny white robes and masks, and we got a bit more daring.

Finding a good hiding place, we waited for them to show up for their usual meeting.

"Here they come," my cousin said. He aimed his gun and shot at the back of one of the members. It was a hit and must have stung, because the guy whipped around to see what had happened. Seeing nothing, he turned back to what he was doing.

It was hard not to fall over laughing. It was just too funny to watch these guys' reactions. We shot a few more members, who had similar reactions. But there was no way we wanted to be found out, so we didn't press our luck. Once the night brought darkness to cover our retreat, we headed back home, feeling a bit devilish.

The next few weeks we continued harassing the KKK members. It was our only real entertainment and got our adrenaline going. We never got caught, at least not at first. It was the excitement of the possibility of getting caught, mixed with the drug taking, that kept us going. I think it went on for nearly a year until the one time we got careless. We were feeling no fear, having dropped some acid before heading off to the sawmill, and we threw all caution to the wind.

Little did we know that the KKK members, tired of being harassed, were on the watch for us. We hid as usual and had our BB guns ready. This time we aimed for their heads. Boy, were they pissed, and as it turned out, they had a good idea of where we had been hiding out all this time.

They started coming for us, and we took off running. My brothers lit off for the mountains, which was the way we usually left, while my cousin and I headed toward the railroad tracks. At first, this seemed like a good idea, but as we soon found out, it was a big mistake. The KKK members hopped in their truck and caught us at the crossing.

"Get down on your bellies," one of the guys shouted at us. He had a gun aimed at my head.

"Don't shoot me," I cried, shaking with fear. I lay down, expecting to be shot in the back. The ground was hard and cold.

"Shut up," he said to me. Then he asked another member, "Did someone take the dogs after the other two that ran up the mountain?"

My heart sank and I started to sob. I had learned that year what the KKK did to people and figured I had little time to live. Not only that, my younger brothers and my cousin would all die with me.

Trouble Strikes

My hands were tied behind my back and I was lifted to my feet. Then one of the men tied a blindfold around my head and marched me to the truck. Two guys lifted me up into the back of the truck and threw me next to my cousin. I could hear him whimpering and I felt extra bad. He was only fifteen, and being the oldest, I felt responsible for him and my two brothers. I began silently praying that they had gotten away, escaped the men's dogs.

One of the members of the KKK sat next to us, then the truck took off down the bumpy country road with us bouncing in the back like sacks of potatoes. It seemed like we traveled quite a distance before the truck finally stopped. The men hauled us out of the back and into some sort of building that smelled like an old barn. They sat us down on some hay and I heard more whimpering from my cousin and knew he was beside me. I grew even more scared when they tied us together with rope. I had heard of lynching and figured we'd be hung from the rafters right there in the barn. I knew no one would ever find us way up there. My parents would sure have a fit wondering whatever had become of us. Maybe we would be left to rot, hanging in that barn.

"What are we going to do with these kids?" I heard one of them say.

"We could whip them and then hang them," was the response.

There was more talk about what they would do to us,

and the more that was said, the more we sobbed in fear. They kept going on like this, and I think they just did it to watch us cry, kind of like a torture before the killing.

Then one of the guys asked me what my name was and I told him.

"Your dad work in the mine?" he asked.

"Yes, he used to. He's retired now," I said and told him my father's name. As soon as I said the words, a new fear struck me. What if they went after my parents?

"I know him," he said to the others. "We worked together in the coal mine a few years back." He turned back to me. "We'll let you all go. Just leave the blindfolds on until you count to a hundred. Then you can go. If you undo the blindfolds early, you're dead. Understand? And don't ever come back here."

He undid our ropes, and I rubbed my wrists and stretched my legs. Although I longed to stand up and get out of there, I dreaded to think of what would happen if I moved an inch.

I heard them walk out of the barn and close the door. Then the truck started, along with some other vehicle, and I heard them fade into the distance. Even though we thought they had all left, we remained still for a while, just in case one of them had stayed behind.

In fact, we were so scared that I think we counted to a hundred twice just to make sure. Then we took the blindfolds off and I saw my brothers, sitting not three feet away from me. I didn't know how they had gotten to the barn, and at that moment, I didn't care. I just thanked God that they were safe. I stared at the ropes hanging from the rafters and started to shake. We came so close to being at the end of them. We looked around the barn and, seeing no one around, we headed slowly for the door. There was no one outside either.

"No one here," one of my brothers said. "Let's get outta here."

We lost no time heading down the road to where we thought home would be, then we took off running like scared rabbits. Before long, though, we ran out of breath and slowed to a walk. It took us the rest of the night and the next day before we found our valley again.

My father asked us where we had been, and when we told him, he asked around to find out who could have done this. No one ever admitted to the incident and we left it alone. We never went back to the sawmill again, and the ordeal stayed with me for quite a while. Eventually, I began to feel better, and thought that might be the end of my troubles. That is when I met the Banton brothers.

Once I turned nineteen, I started driving around in a beat-up old mustang with a couple of friends. While I was cruising around one evening, I saw these guys hitchhiking on the side of the road. One of my friends said he knew them, so I figured we would give them a lift. But as soon as they got into the car, I realized something about them wasn't right. I should have known better than to pick up hitchhikers, but I wasn't thinking that night.

They wanted me to drive them up into the mountains and drop them off up there. Said they were going to get some weed. Sounded reasonable at the time, so I dropped them off up in the hills and they gave me some money for my trouble.

No harm done, I thought as I drove back home.

Several days later, I was listening to the news. When I heard the Banton brothers were arrested for murder, I sat up in my chair.

"Oh, my god!" I started to think about the night I had driven them up into the hills. Was I now an accessory to the crime? My heart dropped down into my boots. The cloud of doom had once again settled around my head. I had to find out more.

I called my friend who'd said he knew the brothers to ask him about it.

"What happened?" I asked.

"They chopped a guy's head off at the railway tracks, couple days ago. Seems they were after his money, but when they found out he didn't have any, they got mad and did him in." My friend told me all the gory details. I was shocked, to say the least.

"Was that the same guy they were going to see for weed that night?" I asked.

"Yep. Same guy. They were actually after his money, not

weed."

"Oh, shit," I said. "Is that when they killed him?"

"No. They went up there a couple times looking for the guy and the last time they found him walking home by the tracks. I guess they were mad that he didn't tell them where the money was. Or maybe he really didn't have any."

"They're crazy," I said.

I let it go at that, but I was so worried, I couldn't eat dinner that night.

"What's the matter, son?" my mom asked as she looked at me suspiciously. I had never refused a meal before.

I told her about what I'd heard on the news and that I had given the guys a ride a few nights before. She shook her head at me in frustration. It seemed like I was the cross she had to bear every day—a thorn in her side. I don't think either of us expected what would take place after that, but we certainly felt something was wrong.

Sure enough, the next day the police came to arrest me as an accomplice.

"I wasn't there," I protested. "I don't even know the guys much at all. Just met them."

"They said you dropped them off," explained the police. "That makes you an accomplice."

I looked at my dad and remembered when as a small boy I'd been taken from the only family I had ever known. This was another time and a different circumstance, but it felt the same. I was hoping my parents could come to the rescue and keep me from going to jail. But my real parents were just as helpless as my adopted family had been all those years ago. My mother was in tears and dad sat motionless in his chair, shoulders drooped.

Seeing the state I was in, he said, "Don't worry, son. We will get a lawyer. The good Lord will see us through." I just hoped he was right. At the moment, it all seemed hopeless.

We couldn't really afford a good lawyer, but dad managed to get one anyway. The lawyer was pretty rough with me, trying to cross me up into making a confession. I knew I had nothing to do with the crime and stuck to my story. My friend was also imprisoned for the same thing. When the Bantons' trial began, things looked pretty bad, with a judge who wanted to send us all to the electric chair and a jury full of white folks who didn't seem to care at all about the black race. It sure was tough to stay in jail during the trial. I was sure no one was listening to me or believed my innocence. My mother came to visit me that month, but she couldn't take the court appearances well and decided to stay at home. My father, though, attended every one. He tried to remain calm, and sometimes I could hear him whisper a prayer, believing that God would not let us down. I was scared as shit with the whole thing.

We were waiting for the Banton brothers to testify and say I had nothing to do with the murder. Hopefully then I would be released from jail. A month went by before the Bantons finally took the stand. Sure enough, they

Trouble Strikes

confirmed my story and I was finally let out of jail. It felt like I had been in there for years. While I was happy to get out of there, I knew my problems were not over. My release was only conditional. At any time, I could be rearrested and charged as an accomplice. The case would go on for a whole year, with me never knowing what the outcome would be. The prosecutor, who didn't like black folks, kept trying to get us all accused of murder, and with that hanging over me, there was no way to get my life settled.

Finally, a verdict came in. The Banton brothers were found guilty and sentenced to death, and the case against me was dropped. Even as my family was celebrating, I was shaken up real bad, thinking how close I'd come to getting the chair myself.

Knowing I had to move on, I tried to find a job, but there was none to be had. My father didn't want me to work the coal mine. He was suffering from black lung and didn't want us kids to have the same problem when we got older.

It didn't help any that a lot of people in town saw me as the kid who was in jail for murder, even though I had been released. No matter how many times I'd told them I had nothing to do with the murder, no one wanted to hire me. I felt stuck and not very confident in myself. In fact, I stayed hidden in the house most of the time.

I did see some old friends, however; they had left to join the military and were now home on leave. They looked so sharp in their uniforms and seemed so sure of themselves. Folks treated them with respect, and they held their heads up high. It got me to thinking: if I joined the military, I would have work and perhaps be trained in some professional job. I would be well thought of and respected. It seemed like a way to get out of the rut I had gotten myself into.

Talk about jumping out of an oar-less boat and into a lake full of alligators.

Chapter Nine
Military Misadventure

As appealing as joining the military seemed, it was still a big decision. When my cousin Lonnie and my friend Tom told me they were joining, it made it easier for me to sign up as well. We all went off to the recruit office together to fill out all the paperwork. When that was all done, we were given a week to pack our things and say goodbye to family and friends.

On the day we left, a van came to the recruit office to pick us up and take us to the airport. Boy, was I nervous! Once on the plane, I ordered a drink to calm myself down, and that led to another one soon after. By the time we landed, I had downed quite a few drinks and was buzzed, as were my friend and cousin. No one seemed to notice as we stumbled across to the Greyhound bus that would take us to the army base.

The trip seemed longer than it actually was, and I was beginning to have doubts about my decision to join. However, I shoved it aside, thinking anything would be better than the life I was living on the pig farm.

When we got off the bus, a drill sergeant was waiting. He started yelling the moment our feet hit the ground. "You guys, get in line, now. What are you, tourists? Are you queers? What?"

We hurried to form some kind of line, but I'm sure we looked pretty pathetic. He walked over to the first guy and, shoving his face close to the new recruit, shouted, "Where you from, boy?"

The recruit stammered, "I'm from Kentucky, sir."

"Texas?" the sergeant yelled, the words spitting out of his mouth. "Nothin' but steers and queers in Texas."

"No, sir," the recruit said. "I'm from Kentucky." He shuffled his feet.

"You're all steers and queers in Kentucky," the sergeant said as he moved on to the next guy in line to repeat the whole thing over again.

Once he had us all shaking in our shoes, he shouted, "Is this what you call a line? You guys are nothin' but pansies. Let's see you all do fifty pushups. Right now!"

We dropped to the ground and started doing pushups. I was in good shape, so I had no trouble doing them. But there were others who couldn't, and the sergeant sneered at them. "Anyone think they can't make it here, get back on the bus."

A few of the guys did get back on the bus, thinking they were getting a ride back home. That didn't happen,

Military Misadventure

though; instead, the sergeant hauled them off and roughed them up well. I could tell he was trying to break us down, and I figured I could handle it, if I was scared shitless. It was definitely hard core.

When we finished our pushups, he yelled at us to pick up our bags and march to the hospital for checkups. The day continued this way, with him screaming orders and insults. Just when we thought it would never end, it was time for dinner. By 8:00, it was lights out, and not a moment too soon. Good shape or not, I was completely exhausted by that time. I practically collapsed onto my bunk, not even caring that my cousin had been assigned to a different platoon.

Bootcamp was hard to get used to. Each morning began with the sergeant screaming at us, followed by the sounds of the trumpet.

"What is this all about?" I asked the guy next to me as I flew out of bed that first morning.

"Don't ask. You have only fifteen minutes to get everythin' done and we're outta here, runnin'."

Didn't take me many days to catch on, because if I didn't, I was in trouble. In those fifteen minutes, I had to be dressed, have my locker looking neat and my bunk made perfectly, among other things. We were then marched out to the pitch field, where we started our day with a five-mile run. By the time that was done and we had run up to the mess hall, I was exhausted. I ate what I could and we were back out drilling some more.

The bootcamp was supposed to last only seven weeks, but when I took the education tests, I failed the math. I would spend the six months going to school to learn the math I was missing, instead of doing bootcamp.

I had been there for about five months when one day I came out of the shower and noticed this guy looking me over. I felt strange and started thinking he might be gay. Since he was a specialist and ranked higher than the rest of us, I thought it better to not say anything to anyone. Might just be my imagination. But then he was there every time I came out of the shower, obviously looking at me. What made matters worse was that I was always scheduled last to take a shower.

After a few days of this, I decided to ignore him and go about my business. That evening, I went to bed as usual. I fell asleep almost immediately, tired after another long day of studying. Sometime later, I was dreaming of wrestling a bear or some large animal, and it woke me up. I found this guy lying on top of me, touching me intimately. Angrily, I threw him off me and jumped out of bed, getting ready to punch his brains out. He ran off and I tried to catch him, but he disappeared into the night. There was a Mexican fellow standing nearby who must have seen it happen, but he didn't want to get in trouble, so he acted like he never saw it. It made me so pissed; I couldn't sleep for the rest of the night.

The next morning, the guy was there in the mess hall, still staring at me. I was so embarrassed I could hardly eat anything. My studies didn't go well that day either. I felt so confused and hurt that a fellow military guy would do this to me. It didn't occur to me to report him.

"What's with this guy staring at me?" I finally asked another student.

"He's gay," was the reply. "Don't pay any attention to him."

I felt disgusted by the whole thing but didn't know what to do about it. Talking to another person about it didn't come easy, so I left it alone.

A few nights later, I woke up again to find him at my bed. I tried to fight him off, but this time he was ready for my reaction. He was very strong and quickly pinned me down.

"You better not say anything to anyone," he whispered, "because no one will believe you."

I could not even believe what was happening to me. It did not even seem real. But it was real, and from that night on, it would continue a few times a week. I had never felt so powerless in my life. I was relieved when I finished school and was told I'd be sent to another location. I thought I would finally be rid of my abuser. To my horror, I was placed nearby, where he could get to me easily. To make matters worse, another person who had been sexually abused by this specialist had now openly accused him. I told him that it had happened to me as well.

"You gotta say something," he would tell me.

I thought if I did, I would surely get into trouble, not to mention the fact that the mere thought of talking about it was unbearable. On the other hand, I knew I could not let this go on forever.

Finally I did complain to an FBI agent who was on the base. I had no idea what would happen as a result, but I figured my attacker would receive some sort of disciplinary action. Well, maybe that would have happened in the civilian world, but this was the military, and the guy was a specialist.

Incredibly, he didn't seem to think he was doing anything wrong; he even approached me several times to invite me to his parties! I never went, of course, I just hoped and prayed that eventually my complaint would be heard by the right people.

Nothing happened right away, though, and I did the only thing I could—worked and drilled as any recruit in boot camp. I had pretty much given up hope when one day, while I was at the shooting range practicing my gun skills, I was called into an office to talk to a private investigator. Outside the office sat two officers staring at their feet. No one said anything to me, and right then and there I felt the nervousness coming on. A lady in uniform sat behind the desk.

"Come in, Mr. Phillips. Have a seat." She pointed

solemnly to a chair across from her.

I sat and she began to ask questions, which I answered as honestly as I could. It was odd that she didn't even blink an eye at what I said. I thought that maybe this was of no surprise to her. Or maybe she didn't really care but was just doing her job. In any case, she finished writing up what I said and dismissed me from the office.

"We'll have to do some investigating," she said. "Then it will have to go to court. We'll let you know."

I left feeling a bit more optimistic that justice would be done. It was only a few more days until an officer came to tell me about the outcome of the investigation. It was still early morning and I had slept well. My spirits were up, and I thought that finally someone understood just what was going on.

"Mr. Phillips?"

"Yes," I said, feeling full of confidence.

"You goin' home."

"What?" I asked, completely shocked.

"Pack your bags. We're coming back for you in twenty minutes." The officers left, and I stood there for a few minutes, staring at the door. I then realized they were coming back and I had packing to do. I went to work collecting my things.

They came back and took me over the warehouse to turn in my gas mask and uniforms. We then went to some office, where they left me to sit in the waiting room, contemplating what had just happened. I was stunned. Didn't I have to be present for the court case? Or wasn't there going to be any? In a way, I was glad to be going home, but somehow this didn't seem right. Did that mean I was to be discharged dishonorably? Or was I going on leave? Did I wear civilian clothes or a uniform? I waited without any real answers until nearly 5:00.

Finally, the officers were back. There was nastiness in their voices as they ordered me around, and I could tell they were mad at me. None of this made any sense. Maybe they were gay too and were covering up for the specialist? I didn't dare ask.

"Here is your pay." One of the officers handed me some cash.

"Only sixty dollars?" That was clearly not enough.

"Yes," he said. "You have to pay for the gas mask."

"I turned it in just now," I protested.

"Says you lost it, on this form," the officer said. "Do you have any paperwork that says you turned it in?"

I started to search my stuff and then realized that I hadn't been given any paperwork.

"They didn't give me any," I said.

"Well, you gotta have paperwork or you pay."

I was dumbfounded. "Did they give me bus money to get home, at least?"

"No. You're on your own."

"What about my discharge papers?" I asked, still trying

Military Misadventure

to piece it all together.

"Sent to the Kentucky office," he said. "Come on, Phillips. You've got a bus to catch."

When we got to the bus terminal, I had just enough for the ticket, and that was all. I hadn't eaten all day, and my stomach was starting to turn somersaults. But I had no extra cash for that and would have to wait until I got home.

Sitting at the bus station, I started to get pissed off. What was I going to do? And what would my dad say? He was counting on me being in the military. He said it was one less mouth to feed and one less son to worry about getting into trouble; he said I liked to party too much. How would the rest of the town treat me? And what was I to say? I felt like my whole life had deflated.

When I got home later that evening, my father asked me what was happening. He thought I might have gone AWOL or worse. I told him I was discharged, and I could see him seething inside.

"Where is your paperwork?" he asked.

"Coming to the office of the Harlan National Guards," I said.

Within the week, my dad took me into Harlan to the National Guard to demand my discharge papers. There were none there. We went several times, and the last time we went, we were told to stay off the property or they would call the police. I had no choice but to wait for someone to contact me.

In the meantime, everyone in our small town knew that I had come home mysteriously, and the rumor spread that I had done wrong. I couldn't tell anyone what had really happened to me in the military. They began to make fun of me whenever I stepped out of the house, and it was not at all pleasant for me. Sometimes I ended up fighting with them. I began spending most of my time in the house, not wanting to see anyone. I had tried to make my life better, only to have everything go back to the way it was after the murder trial.

On Sundays, I went to church with my family. But when I got home, I either stayed in the house and watched TV until I felt I was going crazy, or I went into the hills out back to drink beer or smoke cigarettes or weed. My parents were staunch Christians and would have frowned on smoking or drinking of any kind, so I had to keep it all a secret. During the week I cut wood, which made me just enough money to support my habits. Drinking and getting high were the only way of getting the sexual abuse out of my mind.

Little did I know it was only making things worse. I wasn't getting rid of my anger, just pushing it down inside, and it was only a matter of time before I exploded. I still occasionally went into town and tried to get a job, but no one would give me a chance. I wasn't sure if it was the military discharge or because, by that time, I had very

Military Misadventure

little confidence in myself. It got to be that when I filled out a job application, I wouldn't mention my military experience. But then they would ask me if I had ever been in the military, and when I told them, they wouldn't hire me.

Finally, we were told that my discharge papers had come to the office in Harlan. I was so curious to see what they would say. I thought it would be something positive. We were also waiting to hear about the outcome of the sexual abuse case, and despite everything, I still hoped we would get good news.

We went to get the papers, and it was with shaking hands that I tore open the envelope and read it. It said I was given an "uncharacterized discharge." There was nothing good or bad about it, actually. It just meant that I had only been in the military for 180 days or less and just didn't make it one way or the other. Didn't infer anything bad, but it stung just the same. I could have made it in the military if that specialist had left me alone. Now it didn't even seem like he would suffer any of the consequences that I was suffering. I was shunned by everyone here in town and couldn't even get a job. There wasn't even notice of the court case that I was told would happen.

It got even worse when my cousin and friend came home dressed in greens. Next to them, I looked and felt like nothing, and no one in town let me forget it. I felt trapped and wanted to get away from everything and everyone in that valley. Sometimes, my life didn't even seem worth living.

I had another friend, John, who came to see me once in a while, and we would meet up in the woods to smoke weed or drink beer. One day, he said something that picked up my ears.

"Hey, Garry, why don't we get outta here and go into Lexington? Bet we could get some work and live a lot better than we are here."

It sounded a whole lot better, and I couldn't wait to get out of Dodge. I packed what little I had and we headed down the road, getting a ride from someone going into Lexington. Somehow, I didn't even consider that winter was just around the corner and we had no money and no place to go. We just leaped into the future on blind faith.

We got to Lexington, and as night was coming on, we began to realize our mistake of not making plans first.

"Cold out here," I said. "Where are we going to spend the night?"

He looked at me as if I had some trick up my sleeve; maybe I knew someone we could go to. But I knew no one.

We saw a bridge up ahead and walked over to it, thinking we would huddle in some corner, keep warm until daybreak. There were already several homeless people there, and they had little cardboard tents crudely set up to protect them against the autumn chill.

One of them walked over to us and said, "Yo' guys

Military Misadventure

gonna need some boxes to keep yo'selves warm. Go get yo'self some at the top o' the bridge behind that sto'."

Sure enough, we found some big boxes in a cardboard dumpster and carted them back down under the bridge. We set up camp off to the side, as we hardly knew the other guys. It was definitely warmer for now, but another thing started to bother us. We'd brought some food from home but ate it all on the ride to Lexington. Now we were starving again.

I walked over to the guy who had helped us earlier and asked, "Hey, do you have a way to get food down here?"

"My name is Jack," he said and gave us a toothless grin. "Can't really order pizza delivery." He gave a chuckle and added, "Go up thar behind the McDonald's and dig in the dumpster. Yo'll find some stuff they throw out in the night. Still pretty good when yo' hungry."

John and I introduced ourselves to him and to others who had come over to see what was going on. Didn't say where we came from or what we were there for, just in case these guys couldn't be trusted. Then we hiked back up to the street level to check out this dumpster behind McDonald's. Sure enough, there were some hamburgers and cold fries that had just been tossed out, and we ate until we could burst. Food had never tasted so good, even if it came from a dumpster.

We spent the next few nights under the bridge and the days looking for work. After that, we started to look grubby, and I imagine we stunk too, seeing that we had no bathtub. We gave up looking for work and decided to wait until spring. Some fall days were a bit warmer, and we would sneak down to the river and take a bath early in the morning before too many people were out. This was nice until it got too cold. Then we just got dirtier and dirtier, and smellier too.

Sometimes, when it got too cold, we walked up to the library to get warm. People would look at us in disgust, like we were bums, and I guess we were. I was totally embarrassed and couldn't look at them. I felt dirty and degraded. Someone must have complained about us, because after only a few times in the library, they kicked us out. We had no choice but to go back under the bridge and try to stay warm among the stacks of cardboard.

The snow came too soon and it got even colder. By that time, we had gotten hold of some blankets, and we huddled in our shelters waiting for the warmer days, coming out only to visit McDonald's for our usual hamburgers and fries. Once in a while, we would find chicken and even an apple pie or two. Spring came eventually and the warmer days were encouraging. But the nights were still cold, and we began to light fires under the bridge in order to stay warm.

It didn't take long for the police to see the smoke and come to investigate. When they saw us there, they told us we had to leave. I wondered where we would go, but the police were kind enough to send us to a shelter for the coming night. We had to be there by three in the afternoon; they would give us a hot meal, access to a shower, and cots to sleep on in a huge gymnasium. At six in the morning they would chase us all out and lock the doors. I guess that was so they could clean the place up. It was definitely warmer and the afternoon meals were good. Kept us going until we could eat again the next afternoon.

They also gave us some clean clothes, which meant we could go out again and look for work. We went to Temporary Manpower and stood on the corner. People would drive by and pick out some workers for whatever job they needed them for. John and I didn't get chosen right away because no one knew us. Then, after several days of standing on the corner, our chance came. A guy from the stables at Red Mile Horse Track needed some people to groom the horses. We jumped at the opportunity and went off with him to our first job. The pay wasn't much, but it was steady work, which we needed.

It was also pretty hard work. The bosses could be very demanding, and we were sometimes held responsible for things that were out of our control. One day, I was put in charge of a horse that had injured his leg. My job was to bathe the leg with warm water. I asked a fellow worker to turn on the water but to not make it too hot. Well, he didn't listen, and when it hit the horse's leg, the horse took off running. It ran onto the track and started racing with the other horses, which spooked them all and caused a lot of confusion. People lost money on their bets, and Red Mile had to call the race and refund all the money. I wasn't popular that day.

Once we had saved up enough money, John and I moved out of the shelter and into a rooming house, which was a whole lot more comfortable. We could come and go as we pleased. The room was a bit bare and drafty at times, but for someone like me, who lived most of his life in places even worse, it was certainly a step up. Once we had settled in, I called my family to let them know I was okay.

We had been working at the stables for eight or nine months when one day John came running up to me. I had just started combing a horse's mane.

"Hey, Garry, the restaurant is looking for dishwashers and busboys, and the pay is better. Let's go check it out. I'm tired of this horse groomin'."

I was tired of working with the horses too, and was eager for a change. We applied for the busboy job and started the next week. It was a fancy place and the money was definitely better. Best part was, we got to eat for free.

Even though things were going well, I couldn't get the court case out of my head. Nothing ever came in the mail, and my dad didn't hear anything about it either. Looked like the military had swept it all under the rug and left me to flounder around like a fish out of water. No one seemed to care that I had been violated, and while trying to serve

Military Misadventure

my country.

Most days, I just went to work and tried not to think about it. I enjoyed working at the restaurant and probably would have stayed there, but then something happened to change all that. One day, I was asked to go downstairs and help with the dishes, which I did. When I came for my next shift, the owner accused me of stealing some money he kept in the basement. I knew nothing about it and told him so, but once again I was not believed. After all, I had gone down there to work the day before. I was arrested and put in jail, where I spent a few days. Turns out, the money hadn't been stolen at all; he had just misplaced it. When he found it, I was released, but he never once thought to offer an apology.

I wasn't about to continue working there after that. Instead, applied for a job as a dishwasher at Turf Catering, another racetrack restaurant, and got started washing dishes. It was a rough job, but the pay was good, and I was soon promoted to be in charge of the twenty-person dishwashing crew, which was pretty cool.

The only drawback was that it was seasonal, lasting only during the horseraces, so I had to get other work in between. It didn't take long to find a job at a construction company, and John and I worked with the cleanup crew, stripping off metal and even walking the beams and drilling holes. They were rough jobs, but we got trained pretty good, and we made good money.

During the racing season, I would bet a small amount on the races—sometimes I even won. Those were the better days. But I still had the military experience haunting me and even invading my dreams, and I often didn't sleep so well. I never heard from the military about it, and my father, whose black lung disease was worsening, rarely checked with the National Guard anymore.

Then one winter day, John and I got laid off from the construction crew. We went home and sat watching TV, wondering what else we could do to earn money. It was cold and harder to find jobs at that time, and we were worried. Then we met Ralph. He lived upstairs from us, but we'd never talked to him much as we were always so busy working.

"Yo' all wanna make some real dough?" he asked us one day after we got to talking. "I gotta connection to some cocaine we can sell. Yo' all can make a lotta money selling cocaine."

John and I thought about it. It would help us get through the winter, and then we could find us another job. So we started selling the stuff and made money to pay our bills. When a customer didn't have the cash, we would make a deal with them: let us have your credit card and you can have as much cocaine as you want. We'd just take it off their card by using it to buy clothes, food and stuff we needed. Sounded like a good deal, and we ended up with a good number of credit cards.

But as luck would have it (and I didn't have much luck back then), I would soon end up with the short end of the stick once again.

A Coal Miner's Son

Chapter Ten
Trouble Revisited

Taking and dealing drugs was my big mistake. What had started out as a way to escape the awful memories of the sexual abuse ended up dragging me down to the bottomless pit of despair. The next few years were a series of catastrophes involving women and drugs.

I was twenty-seven years old when I sold cocaine and kept those credit cards of the buyers who couldn't pay. As usual, I was challenging trouble, and as usual, trouble came knocking. One day, I opened the door to find police officers standing there. They wanted to inspect our place.

"We don't have no drugs," I said, confident that we had sold all that we had, and they wouldn't find any.

"You boys are right," the police said, after searching the place, "but what are you doing with all these credit cards?" He spread them all out in his big hand like playing cards.

I had forgotten all about them. They had been sitting in a desk drawer all this time. I tried to explain but the words all came out wrong, and my friend told me to shut up as I was getting us into more trouble.

"Come with me," the officer said, and we all drove down to the police station.

Again we ended up in jail, but this time we were released after one week with orders not to leave town. But after what I'd been through during the Banton trial, I was terrified of ending up in jail again, this time for God knew how long. We headed out of town real quick. I just wasn't thinking right; I guess all the drugs were making me stupid or something.

I was okay for a while out in West Virginia. Made money again by selling drugs, this time carrying a pistol for protection. Sometimes I would get into fights, and there were other times when I robbed a place to feed my own drug habit. I was addicted by this time and couldn't get by without them. I had also lost a lot of weight. Instead of my normal one hundred and seventy-five pounds, I now weighed eighty-five.

One day, a friend of mind showed me an ad in the paper. Someone from Ethiopia needed a green card and was willing to marry someone in the US to get one.

"Why don't you do this, Garry?" he suggested. I jumped at the idea of making ten thousand dollars for myself, and so I answered the ad.

Didn't take long for the girl to arrive and for us to get married. I got my money, and I was settled for a while, taking drugs and just hanging out with the guys. I was also drinking heavily as well. The girl was fine but not one I took a liking to, and I think she felt the same way about me, so we divorced a year later, right after she got her green card.

Then I met another girl that I did take a liking to. She was a user, too, so we ended up high a lot. As I said earlier, drugs and trouble just seemed to be a natural part of my life. Now I was adding women to the mix, and I got double the trouble. The girl needed money for something and stole whatever I had. I was pissed, and when I saw her next, I started beating on her. She didn't have much of a chance with me swinging my fists, but fortunately for her, another guy stepped in and pulled me off her. The police came to check out the fight and, of course, had to check my records.

"Mr. Phillips," said one of the officers, "I see there's a warrant for your arrest in Kentucky."

"What's that for, sir?" I asked, genuinely puzzled.

"Jumping bail," he said. "You have something here about credit card fraud."

That's when I remembered the credit cards, and the cops telling me not to leave Kentucky. Now I'd be headed back there in cuffs.

Luckily, I just got a slap on the wrist and was soon headed back to West Virginia. It was there that I met the girl of my dreams, or so I thought, and got married. My wife had a little girl from a previous relationship, but right from the start, I loved her like she was my very own daughter. We decided to quit the drugs and do the best we could by her. I started to truly believe that life was going to get better.

By that summer, I had cleaned up my act quite a bit and was no longer using. I had a job cutting grass for a lawn service company and was making money to support my family. I was more content with myself than I'd been in years, living honestly in my house with my wife and daughter. Seemed like I had it made.

One day, I came home from work, dirty and sweaty from cutting grass, and prepared to take a shower. My wife had gone out with our little girl, and I was free to just sit and watch some TV until they came back. I took my time with the shower and, feeling pretty good, I grabbed a snack from the fridge and turned the TV on.

There was a loud knock at the door, and I shot out of my chair. The only people I knew who knocked like that was the police, and I wondered what in hell they wanted. I thought I was all done with trouble and was not expecting anything.

"Hi, Garry." It was an officer I knew quite well, along with five others. I invited them in.

"What's up, sir?" I asked, scared that something had happened to my family.

"We have to take you downtown to the precinct," he said.

"What for?" I had to know before I would go with them.

"Well," the officer began, "your wife is accusing you of molesting your daughter."

"What!" I shouted in disbelief. "You know I would never touch her like that. That's crazy."

I was again reminded of the abuse I had suffered in the military. There was no way that I would do anything like that to anyone. Was this a joke? I turned to look at the officer to see if he was playing a joke on me. He was serious and didn't even crack a smile.

"That's what she claims," he said, "true or not."

I sat down hard on the kitchen chair and stared at the table. *How could this be? Do they have the right guy? The right family? What are they talking about?*

"You know I wouldn't do anything like that," I said, breaking the silence after a bit. "You know that."

"I know you, Garry. I don't think you would, but we can't take a chance with this sort of thing. You'll have to come down to the precinct," he said.

It felt like the whole roof had collapsed on my head. This whole idea of being accused unjustly brought back the military affair, the Banton brothers' murder and every other moment of unjust accusations, including some of the whippings I got as a child.

Was I some sort of scapegoat, or was it the choices I was making in life?

I locked up the house and followed the officers out

to the car. All the way to the precinct, I kept trying to think if I could have done this sort of thing without knowing or remembering it. Impossible. I had no problem remembering the rest of my life. Something like this just wouldn't happen. I would never molest anyone, even in a drunken stupor.

I ended up in jail that day, totally puzzled. Nothing made any sense.

This time in jail wasn't easy. The other inmates gave me a hard time. They hated child molesters and hated me. Sometimes I thought they were going to kill me. Once, I got beat up pretty bad and spent a week in the infirmary.

The court appointed me a lawyer who came to see me a few days after that. I told him the other inmates were harassing me, and I was afraid they would kill me.

"I'll see you get a cell to yourself," he said. "We'll get you out of here as soon as we can."

It was nice to see him. He believed me and knew I wasn't lying. I did get a private cell, and it was better, but I wanted to be released. I was not guilty of anything. It was totally unfair.

However, it was my wife's word against mine and she had gotten my daughter to back her up, so I had no leg to stand on. It seemed I would be labeled the same as that guy in the military, although I never did find out what happened to him.

After about three months in jail, my lawyer came to see

me. He seemed happier than usual, and he told me I would be taken to a certain office up on the mountainside. I was wary but had no choice but to go with the officers.

It was nice to get out on the mountains again, although I had no idea what was happening, and that kinda ruined the pleasantness of the outdoors. We went into a room, and there was my little girl. She had been given crayons and was busy doing what she loved best—coloring. As I walked in, she smiled at me, and my heart nearly burst.

"Tell your daddy what you told us a few minutes ago," a female police officer said to my daughter.

"I tol' her that it wasn't you who did that thing. It was the other guy." My daughter looked up from her coloring and looked me square in the face.

"What?" I could hardly believe my ears. "What other guy?"

"The one mommy tol' me not to tell you about. He's her boyfriend. He's the one that touched me." She returned to her coloring.

I could feel the anger swelling up inside me, about to swallow me up.

"She tol' me to say it was you, but it wasn't."

Right then and there, I wanted to hug my daughter and beat my wife at the same time, but I smothered the conflicting emotions and just let the tears roll down my cheeks instead. Feeling faint, I sat down quickly on a chair so I wouldn't fall over.

"You all right, Mr. Phillips?" A police officer brought me a bottle of water.

I was taken back to my jail cell and the officer said, "We just have to do some paperwork and you're free to go. Might take a day or so."

It did take a day before I was released, and I could hardly wait to get back to my place. Although I didn't want to see my wife, I did want to collect my things and clear out of there to a place of my own.

When I got there, she wasn't home. Probably too embarrassed that she'd caused such a problem for me and got me put in jail. Not to mention that she had a boyfriend to live with anyhow.

I got my stuff and went to live with a friend of mine, as I didn't want to have anything to do with the girl I'd married and would probably soon divorce.

"You know, she's into a lot of drugs these days," my friend told me once got to talking.

"Really?" I was surprised. I thought we had decided to stay clean for the sake of our little girl.

"She's been using for the past year or more," he said.

I shook my head. I didn't know what to say or think. It's hard when you get to trusting someone to find out they aren't the someone you thought they were. That evening, my friend and I sat drinking beer and watching TV. It was good to be out of jail, but I felt at a loss. Even though my wife set me up like that, I still had feelings for her.

So it wasn't a surprise that when she came to me and apologized, I took her back. I was so glad to be home that I didn't realize what a stupid move I was making. That night, she brought out some cocaine, and I was back to being a drug user. This time it seemed like it would never end. I would always be addicted to the stuff. I would always be in trouble.

There was one evening when we had gone downtown together. My wife was totally addicted by then and under the influence most days. I wasn't far behind her. Some girl on the street stopped to talk to me, and my wife got so upset, she fell to the ground, screaming and hollering like I had struck her or something. Sure enough, when the police came to check us out, she accused me of hitting her and away I went to jail… again. I'd given her the benefit of the doubt and now I was paying for it.

I wasn't long in jail, and when I got out, I moved away from my wife. Needless to say, I got a divorce as soon as I could. I wasn't going to get bitten by the same dog twice. Or I guess in this case, three times. Thinking of getting as far away as I could from trouble, I moved to another town, and that's where I met a pastor named Earl.

"I have an extra space in my house," he said after we spoke together, and I had told him what was going on with me. "You can rent that space from me, and I can help you get off the drugs."

Sounded like a good idea for me, and I moved in the

next day.

Living with Earl was like a breath of fresh air. He helped me get off drugs and get straight. We went fishing together and shared our life stories. Those were the good days and I didn't ever want them to stop, even though fishing brought its own challenges.

The fishing place was in a white neighborhood, and in those days, the whites and blacks were still segregated in West Virginia. They didn't much like it that Earl, a white man, was fishing with me, and several times they came to chase us out of the area. Earl wouldn't give in, though, and so we kept coming back to the same area to fish. I trusted that he knew what he was doing, and I felt that I was sort of protected by his presence.

Earl had a cousin, Robert, who lived in the same house as we did, along with his father (Earl's uncle) and mother. One day, Robert came to me with a job offer. His father was dying of cancer and needed a caretaker. His mom was also getting on in years and needed someone to keep an eye on her as well. He would pay me to take care of them. Although I was already working in the laundry department of the local hospital and had some social security, I welcomed the additional income. I was also glad to be in a position to help someone.

"Sure," I told him, somewhat surprised that Robert had come to me at all. He was an ex-KKK member, and although he had changed his views about black people, I

Trouble Revisited

didn't think he would trust one to care for his parents. His father, on the other hand, was still stuck in the old ways, and I think he came to think of me as a slave or at least a servant. But he was happy to have me take him to his doctor appointments, give him his baths and stuff like that, and he often spoke kindly to me. I didn't even mind when he called me the "n" word. I knew that I was doing a good job, and that made me proud of myself and returned to me some of the self-esteem that I had lost so many years ago.

"You know," he said to me one day, "I've never in my life seen such a black man like you work so hard." I cherished that comment to this day. I think he grew fond of me as he neared the end of his life.

He eventually ended up in the hospital, and he called me to his deathbed. "Garry," he said, "gotta tell you, you have taken such good care of me and always been nice in the roughest of times. Sometimes, I wasn't so nice to you and called you names on my worst days. I want to say I'm sorry for that and want to know if you will forgive me." I think he was afraid he would go to the bad place after he died, but it didn't matter to me why he apologized. I was just happy that he had.

"Yes, of course," I said, and I meant it, too. Taking care of these people had given me my life back. I had a job to do and a responsibility, and they depended on me. I couldn't slip up and go back to my old ways.

I took care of Robert, too, in a way. He had been an addict and was on medication for drug and alcohol abuse, and I made sure he had his medication and was doing things right. Sometimes, I was his conscience and kept him out of trouble that would have sent him to jail.

I found that helping these folks kept me on the straight and narrow, too, since I figured that if I stayed strong, then maybe Jesus would help me, too. Becoming a Christian helped me keep in line, also. I cleaned my life up in so many ways. I even got my driver's license back so I could drive the old man around.

Earl and I did a lot of fishing and talking, and I grew to liking the guy quite a bit. He was a good friend to me, and I tried to be a good friend to him as well. The one thing that still bothered me was the folks who called us names when we went fishing or into town. Earl said to not let it bother me, and I tried to keep it away from my thoughts, but it was still in the back of my mind. They even gave us a hard time when we went into restaurants.

For three years we lived the good life, enjoying each day as it came. Then, just when things seemed a little too good, they took a turn for the worst.

"I got bad news for you, Garry," Robert said to me one day, "and you better seat yourself down."

My heart started doing the flutter kick in my chest as I sat down in the kitchen and tried to prepare myself. But nothing could have prepared me for what he said next.

"Garry," he said, with tears welling up in his eyes, "Earl is gone."

"Gone?" I asked. "Where did he go?"

"No," he replied, "Earl is dead."

I felt numb to the very deepest part of me. *How could he be dead?* I wondered. He was very much alive this morning.

"How ... what?" I stammered, at a loss for words.

"The police found him in a burned-up car by the side of the road. They want us to come down for some questioning."

This didn't make sense to me. Earl was not the sort to commit suicide, nor was he a careless man. How could this have happened? We went down to the precinct and answered the questions. I felt like I was buried in a bale of cotton; nothing seemed real to me, and I walked around in a fog.

A few days later, the police called us, asking if Earl had any enemies.

"Why do you ask?" Robert asked the officer.

"Looks like he was beaten in the head and knocked out before being placed in the car and set on fire."

With a jolt, I thought of all the folks who had treated him badly for associating with me. They'd threatened us one day, and I didn't take it seriously. Neither did Earl. Suddenly, I felt totally responsible for his death. Because of me, he was brutally murdered. It was not a good day for me. In fact, the entire week was miserable as we prepared for his funeral. And I kept thinking that if I had been with him that day, I would have been killed, too. It was just not fair for such a good man to have suffered that fate because of me. My heart wrenched in my chest.

At the graveside, I struggled to hold in my tears at the loss of such a dear friend. I also lost the person who had kept me stable for the past three years. What was I going to do now? Where would I go? And how could I get away from this horrible, painful feeling? At least Robert understood and suggested I stay with him for a while at the house until I planned my next move. After the funeral, I walked down to the nearest restaurant, thinking I would pick up something to eat before going home.

"Get out," the owner yelled. "We don't serve your kind here."

I left and went home, completely destroyed. There seemed no place to turn. As the days passed, I became worried that I might be accused of killing Earl. I had had so much bad luck, it didn't seem too far from the truth at that time. Time for me to leave town and go down to Florida, where my brother lived.

Chapter Eleven
Getting Back On My Feet

When I got to Florida, I stayed with my brother for a few weeks. Even though I felt safer, I was still a mess. I could not get Earl's murder out of my head; nor could I forget how I was treated by the folks in West Virginia. How could some people be so kind and others so nasty? It wasn't long before I took to doing cocaine again, just to ease the hurt. In spite of that, I was able to find work cleaning a bakery and soon moved to my own place. I was about forty years old. Looking back, I could see that I had committed at least eight years of my life to crime and maybe even more to doing drugs. Life didn't look like it would get any better, and I felt all the years I'd spent with Earl fly away with his death. I was going downhill fast.

Because of the drugs, I had once again lost a staggering amount of weight and was back down to eighty-five pounds. People often whispered about me, and I knew they thought I was sick, crazy, for both. I thought maybe they weren't far wrong. Life certainly didn't seem worth living, and I didn't know how to stop this fast train speeding into a train-wreck.

I did have a friend, Bobby, with whom I often did drugs. One evening, we climbed up the stairwell of a half-finished building, all the way to the twenty-seventh floor. There, on the open balcony, were other guys we knew—smoking and drinking Knickerbocker beer. Bobby joined them, talking and watching the traffic down below, but I just sat there silently.

It was either the condition I was in or the combination of the drugs and beer that brought me so low that night. All I knew is that I really didn't want to go on. My entire life seemed empty and worthless.

"What's up, Garry?" one of the guys asked. "You are too quiet over there."

"Don't bother him," said another guy, "He's just crazy."

I'd heard people say that about me plenty, but that night, it really hit home. I didn't answer him, just sat for a while, wallowing in self-degradation. Then I stood up and walked over to the concrete railing. No one said a thing as I climbed it unsteadily, staring down at the people below. They were so small and unreal—like I felt at the moment.

The wind up that high was strong, and I could feel it pulling at me, calling me to fly away with it into another place and another time. I began to sway, and I knew I was going over.

Chapter Twelve
Who Was The Man On The Railing?

The man stood on top of the balcony railing, swaying slowly in the wind like a drunken waltz. Twenty-seven stories below, a crowd had gathered on the street after one person happened to look up, see the stick-thin figure about to jump, and began pointing and shouting. A handful of people had pulled out their cell phones and called 911, no one believing he would last that long. Even from far away, they could see the despair in his rounded shoulders and in the way his arms hung slack at his sides. Maybe he wasn't going to jump after all— maybe he was just going to let Death decide if it wanted to take him.

"What would make someone do that?" one man asked, giving voice to the question on everyone's mind.

"Buncha druggies hang out up there," another muttered dismissively. He held up a hard hat to indicate he worked construction on the building. "Prob'ly high as a kite."

His comment drew a sharp look from the woman next

to him, as well as several nods of agreement from others in the crowd. Drugs. It was the simplest, most palatable explanation for what they were witnessing—this very public display of human suffering. What had started as an ordinary day for these folks would become the day they would see a man end up as a crimson stain on the street. It was easier to accept that it was the drugs—rather than the unfairness of life—that had brought him to it.

The crowd gave a collective gasp as the man teetered dangerously forward, about to go over the railing. Some shut their eyes, not wanting to see the end; others moved off to the side, thinking he may land on them. Everyone held their breath.

Just as he reached the point of no return, they saw a hand jut out from behind the man and pull him back off the ledge. "Somebody saved him!" a woman shouted.

"Thank the Lord!" another said, blessing herself with the sign of the cross, then making a steeple of her hands. "Thank you, God!"

The tension that had gripped the crowd for the last several minutes burst, like a balloon pricked with a needle. Everyone turned to each other smiling with relief, bonded in some strange way by the tragedy they had almost witnessed. For the rest of the day, perhaps longer, even the most cynical among them would see their lives in a different light and realize how blessed they were.

As they broke apart, they heard a faint sound coming

from the balcony above. It was laughter, a cackling humor with an edge of relief running through it.

The man holding the hard hat grunted. "Told ya he's one of them damn druggies...."

The younger man glanced up at the balcony again, shaking his head in wonder. "Whoever he is, somebody up there was lookin' out for his ass, and I don't mean his buddy on the balcony, either. Whoever he is, it wasn't his day to die."

The other man grunted again. "He's a lucky bastard, I'll give him that." He placed the hat on his head. "He must be the luckiest sucker in the world."

A Coal Miner's Son

Epilogue
Editor's Note

It's been twenty years since Garry Phillips, high on crack and broken from a lifetime of misfortune, nearly plunged to his death. While many people may have seen it as pure luck that his friend pulled him back from the ledge, Garry saw it as an opportunity to transform his life. He stopped using drugs, and although life has often been hard, he has remained clean ever since. Today, he has a wonderful son and volunteers at the VA, speaking with troubled veterans.

Garry does not claim to know what the future will bring, but he believes the good Lord gave him a second chance for a reason and will continue to help him stay on the path of righteousness. For him, that means sharing his inspiring story with others and hopefully helping them through their own challenges. "It's been a hard road to travel," he said, "and I didn't do it by myself. But I am living proof that with perseverance and faith in God, we can overcome anything."

www.ingramcontent.com/pod-product-compliance
Lightning Source LLC
Chambersburg PA
CBHW070648050426
42451CB00008B/311